the
Bootlegger
Blues

A PLAY BY

DREW HAYDEN TAYLOR

Fifth House Publishers

Canadian Cataloguing in Publication Data

Taylor, Drew Hayden, 1962–
   The bootlegger blues : a play

   ISBN 0-920079-79-2

I. Title.

PS8589.A885B6   1991   C812/.54   C91–097157–9
PR9199.3.T295B6   1991

This book has been published with the assistance of
The Saskatchewan Arts Board and The Canada Council.

Fifth House Publishers
1511-1800 4th Street SW
Calgary, AB
T2S 2S5

Printed and bound in Canada by Friesens
Corporation, Altona, Manitoba

05 06 / 7 6 5 4

the Bootlegger Blues

A PLAY BY

DREW HAYDEN TAYLOR

ACKNOWLEDGMENTS

The Bootlegger Blues is the product of a lot of hard work by many wonderful people. The genesis of the play was workshopped during Native Earth Performing Arts annual Native Playwright Festival workshop, "Weesageechak Begins to Dance," back in 1990.

The play was produced that summer by De-Ba-Jeh-Mu-Jig Theatre Group on Manitoulin Island, where it premiered on the Wikwimikong Unceded Reserve 2 August 1990. *The Bootlegger Blues* toured Ontario for two months with the following cast:

      Justine Enosse—Martha
      Gloria Eshkibok—Marianne
      Dwayne Manitowabi—Blue
      Jani Lauzon—Angie
      Billy Merasty—David
      Clayton Odjig—Noble

      Directed by Larry Lewis
      Costumes and props by Cheryl Mills
      Lights by Kennetch Charlette
      Sets by Cheryl Mills and Kennetch Charlette
      Stage Manager—Jeff Trudeau

The song "The Bootlegger Blues":
      Music by Gary Williams
      Music transcribed by Gerry and Sherry Young,
      Eagle Studios, Saskatoon, SK
      Lyrics by Drew Hayden Taylor

These people are only the tip of the iceberg. The author would like to thank Audrey Debassige for taking me into her home during the rehearsal and production. I'd also like to thank the other people who participated in the workshop: Herbie Barnes, Arlinda Stonefish, Ed Peters, and the indomitable Vinetta Strombergs. Thanks also to Anita Knott, my aunt, for once again providing the Ojibway translations. And finally, to my mother and family, who provided so much material for this story without actually doing anything—just being themselves (those who are still talking to me).

Comedy . . .
What a laugh!

PRODUCTION NOTES

The Bootlegger Blues is a comedy with a lot of movement, so there should be space to maneuver. The original production of *The Bootlegger Blues* contained a set broken up into three areas. The first and busiest was Martha's kitchen, which also doubled as the community center kitchen. It's here, with the fridge full of beer and Marianne cooking actual eggs on stage that the tone of the play was set. It was painted yellow for a domestic tone.

The second area was the space that doubled for all outdoor activities: the powwow grounds, David and Noble's confrontation, Angie and Blue's romantic walk. This background was painted green.

And finally came Blue's bedroom, where the fabulous wall of beer was located, Blue's seduction happened, and David's transformation. For obvious reasons, the room was painted blue.

Scattered throughout the play are occasional passages in Ojibway, the language of the community. These could easily be translated into various other Native languages depending on the whim of the individual theater company.

For atmosphere, there was a working stove on stage, so the audience could hear the authentic sound of eggs frying and smell them as they cooked.

CAST OF CHARACTERS

Martha (the mother)
    —58 years old

Marianne (the daughter)
    —34 years old

Andrew/Blue (the son)
    —24 years old

Angie (the friend)
    —22 years old

David (Marianne's common-law husband)
    —35 years old

Noble (the dancer)
    —34 years old

LOCATION

All the action takes place on a typical, contemporary Indian reserve located in central Ontario.

TIME

Twenty-four hours during a powwow weekend.

ACT I

SCENE I

The scene is a large kitchen found in community centers everywhere. Everything is a mess, showing current use. In the background drum music can be heard. A powwow is going on. Martha, a matronly woman in her late 50s, comes charging like a train into the kitchen, carrying a huge bowl of peeled potatoes.

MARTHA:

How many more orders? (*Pause*) Oh my lord, they want seconds? Tell them to lick their plates till the corn soup's done. I'm getting too old for this. After feeding the first hundred people, I start to get kinda tired. It's amazing the way them dancers can jump around the way they do with so much food in their stomachs. The way they jump and bounce you'd think they were all Rabbit Clan or something. But I gotta keep telling myself, it's for the church. Nobody ever told me peeling potatoes would become God's work.

She starts peeling potatoes, gradually to the beat of the drum.

MARTHA:

Does set a nice pace, though. Music to peel by.

Martha busily peels potatoes. Occasionally she looks with frustration at the clock, as if waiting for someone. Marianne's head appears around the corner. She knows she's late.

MARTHA:

I never should have agreed to do this. It's more work than I ever expected.

MARIANNE:

It's the same with men.

MARTHA:

It might help if you'd try marrying one instead of just shacking up with them. You should marry David, he's so nice.

MARIANNE:

And you should stop smoking. Both would probably kill us. Geez Mom, it's hot in here.

MARTHA:

You better get used to hot places.

MARIANNE:

The hotter the better, Mom. Brownies!

MARTHA:

Get away from that food. If you want some, you know where to buy your ticket.

MARIANNE:

How much food you got in here anyways?

Martha opens up a huge refrigerator door showing an innumerable number of beer bottles.

MARIANNE:

I like your interior decorator.

Marianne reaches for one but Martha closes the refrigerator door before she's successful. Marianne continues to stare longingly at the closed door.

MARTHA:

It's all the fault of that old fool, Marjorie. She told me, (*In a shrill, nagging voice*) "You can't have a dinner for Indians without selling beer, they'll go crazy." Crazy fool, she ain't been the same since she got hit with the ball at that baseball game.

MARIANNE:

Remember Mom, love thy neighbor.

*Martha shoves a big bowl of potatoes into
Marianne's gut.*

MARTHA:
And obey thy mother!

*Marianne finds the bowl extremely heavy and
gradually loses her grip on it.*

MARTHA:
The old bat. So now I got all this beer and I
don't know what to do with it. Being a good
Christian woman like myself, I've never even
taken a sip, never a sip in my life, and never
will. Never even had it in my house.

MARIANNE:
Uh, Mom …

MARTHA:
(*Angrily*) That Marjorie. "I'll fill out the forms,"
she said. "You just have to sign them," she said.
Ever since we was little kids Marjorie never
caused me nothing but trouble.

MARIANNE:
Mamaa, piniig! [Mother, the potatoes!]

MARTHA:
I'd better start getting used to striped pajamas
and bread and water. There probably won't be
any decent good scone there either. All I can do
is pray these powwow people start getting a
powerful thirst soon.

MARIANNE:
You're not supposed to drink and drum, Mother.
The few that drink do it at night, when you're
closed. I told you all this before.

MARTHA:
Bah, it don't matter if it's day or night, drinking
is drinking and if they're gonna do it, it might
as well support the church.

Marianne is visibly straining under the weight of the potatoes.

MARIANNE:
Mamaa, znigziwag giw! [Mama, it's heavy!]

MARTHA:
Dga-binizh giw. [Oh, give me those.]

Martha grabs the potatoes with ease.

MARTHA:
That's the problem with women today, not enough muscle.

MARIANNE:
Finally. Thank you.

MARTHA:
I would have thought that exercise man of yours would have done something good with that body of yours by now.

MARIANNE:
Not in a while, Mom, not in a while.

MARTHA:
I was told them type drink beer—I bought them beer and now they're ignoring me. Ungrateful dancing fools. My mother always warned us liquor would be the ruin of us some day. I didn't think she meant this way. I'm going outside for a smoke. Some of those dishes could use a good cleaning.

Marianne grabs a knife and creeps up on her mother as if to stab her. Martha catches Marianne in the act. Martha doesn't bat an eye.

MARTHA:
And the pots.

Marianne angrily throws the knife into the sink, splashing herself in the process. Martha exits.

MARIANNE:
(*Yelling*) Shit!

Wiping herself, she walks over toward the radio and turns it on.

ANNOUNCER:

It's up to a blistering 28 degrees out there in cottage country. No relief in sight for the remainder of the weekend, so take a bit of advice from Kawartha Radio, grab a cold beer, jump in the lake, sit back and remember the good old days as you cry with me.

The instrumental of "I've Got A Tear In My Beer" starts to play. As she does the dishes, she grabs a spoon and starts belting out the song in Ojibway. This is the real Marianne, a woman who wants to have fun, drink a beer, sing a song, and dirty plates, not wash them.

MARIANNE:

Sabiingway yaamgud maa ndi beerming pii mwiyaan
Miigo pane nsaanandmaan.
Pii shaangswi menkweyaan miigo gaazhi baashk-demyaan

Miigo pane nsaanendmaan.
Nwii gchi mnikwe kopii shkitooswaan ji maajiiyaan
Gnamaa gonaa daa maajaamgodoon niw sabiing-wyaashun
Sbiingway yaamgad maa ndi beerming pii mwiyaan
Miigo pane nsaanendmaan!

Dibikong ngii gchi baamse, naasaab go wasbikong
Miigo pane nsaanendmaan
Endigo eshkwaabmaadziyaan epiichi nshinaad-endmaan
Miigo pane nsaanendmaan
Nga gchi minkwe go dopii maajiisnog sa iw nzidoshs
Gnamaa gonaa gaawiin ndaawiiskikaaksiin iw nde
Subiingway yaamgad maa ndi beerming pii mwiyaan
Miigo pane nsaanendmaan!

Ngii gehi ktaamgoz ji gaadooyaan niw nsabiingwyan
Miigo pane nsaanendmaan
Kina niw ensaanigyaan aashgo ngii pugzikaagnan
Miigo pane nsaanendmaan
Geyaabi go nga mnikwe, gaawiin dash g'gamk-
  wenmisoon
Gaawiin pooch ngiishitoosiin ji nbaayaan iwgaa-
  bimiseg
Sabiingway yaamgad maa ndi beering
  piimwiyaan
Miigo pane nsaanendmaan!

*Martha walks in. Marianne stops in mid-song
but Martha doesn't notice. Embarrassed,
Marianne pretends she was drying the spoon.*

MARTHA:
Marianne Elizabeth, I've made a mountainous
decision. I refuse to go to jail for being sweet-
talked by that Marjorie. Last time I allowed
myself to be sweet-talked, you appeared. (*Opens
the refrigerator*) Look at all this … (*She spits the
word out*) beer. Who cares if I get drummed out
of the Church Recreation Committee, or that the
church doesn't get its new organ? What does it
matter if I'm made a laughing stock of the
village, and that fool Marjorie will hold it over
my head for the rest of my goddamned life—

MARIANNE:
Mama!

*Marianne is astounded. Martha clamps her
hands over her mouth then together in prayer
and looks to the heavens.*

MARTHA:
Oh my goodness, forgive me, Lord. It was the
beer talking. Thank the Lord nobody heard me.

MARIANNE:
I did.

*Suddenly the door swings open and Andrew
jumps through with a flourish. A good-looking,
athletic young man, Andrew has been away at
college for the last five months. He's Martha's
favorite and knows it.*

ANDREW:

Ta da!

MARIANNE/MARTHA:

Andrew!!

*Both Marianne and Martha rush to Andrew and
cover him in hugs and kisses. He is pushed back by
the rush. He enjoys it for a moment then starts to
push them away, trying to salvage his sense of
machismo. During all this, David slips quietly into
the room, carrying a portable typewriter. David is
Marianne's common-law husband, a stuffed shirt
with an overly developed sense of office and life
protocol. He is an Indian yuppie.*

ANDREW:

Okay, that's enough, that's enough. (*To
Marianne*) Geez, God only knows where your
lips have been.

MARTHA:

You watch that mouth of yours, young man.

MARIANNE:

Remember, she's small but wiry

David manages a feeble entrance.

DAVID:

Ta da!

*Martha notices him but Marianne doesn't
acknowledge him.*

MARTHA:

Oh hello, David. (*Back to Andrew*) He looks
thin. Does he look thin to you, Marianne?

MARIANNE:
>I think he's put weight on. Is that muscle in there? Don't tell me they actually make you work at that college of yours, Mr. Soon-To-Be Special Constable.

>*Marianne pokes Andrew affectionately. He tries to fight her off but she outmaneuvers him in the way only a big sister can.*

MARTHA:
>Are you hungry, Blue?

ANDREW:
>Hungry ain't the word, Mom.

MARTHA:
>You poor boy! You must be starving.

>*Andrew shrugs as he grabs a brownie and starts to eat it.*

MARIANNE:
>How come he gets to have a brownie?

MARTHA:
>He's a growing boy.

MARIANNE:
>You never gave me brownies when I was a growing girl.

MARTHA:
>(*Points to Marianne's waist*) You grew without me. When I was your age, I was thin as a rail.

MARIANNE:
>That's because baloney hadn't been invented yet.

DAVID:
>Marianne, can I talk to you for a minute, please? It's business.

MARIANNE:

When isn't it? Look David, today's a holiday. I don't want to even think about work. I just want to go to the powwow.

DAVID:

There are things you have to attend to. We all must abide by the rules. The band office is a finely tuned instrument that must be held together.

MARIANNE:

It's a group of cousins. (*Notices the typewriter*) What's that?

DAVID:

Your date for the powwow.

MARIANNE:

David, no!

Meanwhile, Martha is preoccupied with Andrew.

MARTHA:

(*To Andrew*) You need a haircut, you do, Blue. Definitely need one, eh Marianne?

Marianne begins to answer but is cut off by her mother.

MARTHA:

Are you eating okay in the city?

Andrew starts to answer but is cut off too.

MARTHA:

It doesn't matter. You can eat good here, and rest up too. You look kind of tired.

ANDREW:

It was a long trip. Now that I'm here, is there anything you want me to do?

MARTHA:

Get out. Go have some fun today. There's plenty enough time for work tomorrow.

MARIANNE:

(*Surprised*) What? Let him cut up a turnip or something.

MARTHA:

He'll do no such thing. A man in the kitchen gives me the willies. Blue, remember the time your father tried to roast that chicken in the oven?

ANDREW:

Oh yeah, I remember, but it all turned out for the best. We got to like the new house.

MARTHA:

Get out of my kitchen, young man.

MARIANNE:

Spoiled brat.

ANDREW:

Fine with me. And Marianne, don't work too hard, you know how I worry about you.

Andrew grabs another brownie as he starts to leave.

MARIANNE:

(*Smiles wickedly*) Have all the brownies you want, little boy Blue, have a bunch. I made them special for you.

ANDREW:

Why? What's in them? Are these some of your funny brownies?

MARIANNE:

Of course not. Go ahead, take another one. From a sister to a brother.

ANDREW:

Mom! What did she put in them?

Martha ushers the nervous Andrew out the door.

MARTHA:

Don't pay any attention to her, Blue. Go enjoy yourself. (*She walks by David*) Nice to see you, David.

DAVID:

Thank you, Martha. Cooking heartily I see.

Martha exits carrying some dishes. David spots Marianne trying to sneak out the door.

DAVID:

The report, Marianne.

MARIANNE:

Damn, another four feet and I could've made it.

DAVID:

Marianne, you know the council. Unlike me, they don't have a sense of humor. That computer was a major investment for the office. It was either that or the sauna. They won't stand for another incident.

MARIANNE:

The computer just crashed, that's all. It crashed and there wasn't one single, stupid thing I could do about it.

DAVID:

To most people, crashing a system means losing all their computer programs. To you it means dropping the damn thing on the floor. The band manager insists—

MARIANNE:

For god's sake, his name is Frank.

DAVID:

The band manager insists it be on his desk tomorrow morning by 9 A.M. sharp.

Martha enters with some dirty dishes.

MARIANNE:
But the powwow …

DAVID:
… will have to wait.

Martha plops a stack of dishes in front of Marianne.

MARTHA:
Dishes.

MARIANNE:
But …

MARTHA:
(*Firmly*) Dishes.

Marianne looks sadly at the report, then the pile of dishes.

MARIANNE:
Sometimes I think they breed when they're alone in the sink.

DAVID:
I'm off to run some errands but I'll pop by later to see how you're doing. Good luck, sweetheart.

MARIANNE:
I'll never get out of here. I wonder what the evil stepsisters are doing?

SCENE 2

Angie is standing by the bleachers watching the powwow. Angie is a beautiful 22 years old, and is new to the reserve. She's eating something when she notices Andrew walking in the distance. She recognizes him and is impressed. Wanting to make a good impression, she tries to get rid of the food. She bends over the railing, exposing her behind. Andrew walks over and can't help but notice Angie's position.

ANDREW:
> Well, hello there. I don't believe I recognize you.
>
> *Angie, embarrassed, turns around.*

ANGIE:
> Uh, excuse me?

ANDREW:
> (*Sees her face*) Now I'm sure of it. Don't think I've ever seen you around here. I would have remembered you. What's your name?

ANGIE:
> Who wants to know?

ANDREW:
> I do.

ANGIE:
> And who are you?

ANDREW:
> Who would you like me to be?

ANGIE:
> Somebody six foot four, biceps that could crack walnuts, money enough to buy me all the horses in the world, and every time he comes over to spend the night, he has to bring a shoehorn, if you know what I mean? That's the *big* requirement?
>
> *Andrew is deflated.*

ANDREW:
> Good luck.

ANGIE:
> Don't tell me you give up so quick? What do they call you around here, one shot Blue?

ANDREW:
> Just Blue. How'd you know my name?

ANGIE:
(*Smiles mischievously*) And I can tell you how you got your nickname.

ANDREW:
I don't think so.

ANGIE:
One hot summer you were in quite a rush to go play baseball. In your hurry to do up your pants, you accidently caught a certain part of your anatomy in the zipper of your blue jeans. Pajogeen in the odjee.

ANDREW:
(*Weakly*) P'jogan.

ANGIE:
By the time they unjammed it, you were blue, and a nickname was born.

ANDREW:
It was either that or "Stubby."

ANGIE:
And when you were 14, there was that little incident with the magazines under your bed. I believe you were caught …

ANDREW:
What are you? A witch or something? How do you know this stuff?

ANGIE:
Doesn't everyone?

ANDREW:
Oh god, I hope not. Come on, you bribing my relatives or something? You with the DIA?

ANGIE:
My, aren't we paranoid.

ANDREW:
I'm not paranoid. Who are you?

ANGIE:

I'm a friend of your sisters.

ANDREW:

Marianne? She dies. You don't look like her normal type of friend. No tattoos. Does she owe you money or something?

ANGIE:

Nothing like that. A couple months ago this guy with no front teeth was hustling me at one of the reserve dances. He pissed me off and I started yelling at him for a good five minutes.

ANDREW:

What happened?

ANGIE:

I found out he was deaf in one ear. Then suddenly the famous Marianne who I'd heard so much about was standing at my side.

ANDREW:

I bet he pissed his pants.

ANGIE:

All down the floor. And I haven't seen him since. And now Angie and Marianne rule the village. I even helped her plant her garden, if you can believe that.

ANDREW:

Angie? Angie White?

ANGIE:

(*Surprised*) Yeah.

ANDREW:

As in Bill C–31 Angie White?

ANGIE:

Yeah.

ANDREW:

As in Angie White, age 22. Five feet, five inches, weight normally 120 pounds but rose to 133 since arrival on reserve. Blames lack of proper exercise facilities, but in actual fact due to the introduction of a higher cholesterol diet and a devotion to her Aunt Julia's strawberry pies. Born July 2nd weighing in at seven pounds, two ounces. Very intelligent but for some reason has a fondness for romance novels. Bra size 34 C ...

ANGIE:

Sorry to disappoint you but it's 34 B.

ANDREW:

Damn!

SCENE 3

Marianne is sitting in the kitchen at one end of the stage staring dully at the typewriter.

MARIANNE:

(*Singing*) A-B-C-D-E-F-G-H-I-J, I could sure use a Jay about now. I never noticed how some keys remind me of certain people's faces.

She stabs at some keys vengefully.

MARIANNE:

Ah Frankie, you'd look great with an X across your face. And David, don't get T'd off. (*Pause*) To work or not to work, that is the question. Whether 'tis nobler in the mind to suffer the slings and arrows of outrageous fortune, or go on pogy. Damn that Frankie and David, making me work on a holiday. I'm sick and tired of blisters on my fingertips and calluses on my ass. Just because of a tiny little accident with a $6,000 computer. It was insured. Somewhere out there, women are having fun. Ten years ago I was out there dancing. I was 24, making a fortune renting out my I.D. Ten years, David, the drum's the same but we aren't. We shouldn't have quit the powwow circuit. We lost too much. Look at me, I'm cleaning, cooking, doing reports. I should be out there kicking up dirt, not writing it.

I wonder if Frankie is at the powwow. "It's a charming cultural event, and it might generate some much-needed revenue." It's amazing how a man with such a big neck and head can have no brains.

SCENE 4

Lights come up to illuminate the bleachers as Marianne continues to type. Angie and Andrew listen to the announcer on the loudspeaker.

ANNOUNCER:

Would all contestants for the men's Fancy Dance Competition please move to the dancing area.

ANGIE:

Oh good, more dancing. Just look at all this. Have you ever seen so many Indians in all your life? And they're all dancing and singing.

ANDREW:

You'll find that at powwows occasionally.

Noble enters in his Fancy Dancing outfit. He is 34 and looks quite impressive. He bends over to adjust his leggings.

ANGIE:

Nice buns.

ANDREW:

You like that type?

ANGIE:

He's colorful.

ANDREW:
So's an infected finger.

Noble stands, ready to dance. Marianne works on her report, miserably typing away in the kitchen. After a couple of seconds the sound of the typewriter keys begins to sound like the drum thumping. Then the actual drum comes up and Noble starts to dance. With the first few thumps of the drum, he trembles. The drum song starts up in earnest, and so does Noble. He starts slowly but gradually he's moving faster and faster, with feathers flying. He is in full flight. The music seems to invade Marianne. She looks down at her typewriter. Her face tightens, she stands up, grabs the typewriter, lifts it up, swings it off the desk, then drops it with a loud crash. She smiles a self-satisfied smile. Happily she goes off to see the powwow. She waves to Angie and Andrew. Angie points to Noble and shouts something. Marianne sees Noble dancing and is mesmerized. She watches him for a moment then hesitantly goes to him when the music stops. She touches his shoulder gently, he turns around and she gingerly offers him her pop. He accepts it with a grateful smile. Their hands briefly touch.

MARIANNE:
Thirsty?

NOBLE:
Dryer than a camel's fart.

Noble winks at her. Marianne is almost embarrassed.

MARIANNE:
My friend thinks you have nice buns.

NOBLE:
Oh yeah, tell her to take a number.

MARIANNE:
You're a very good dancer, you know.

NOBLE:

Tell that to the judges. Out there sweating to beat hell for nothing. Barely made gas money to the next powwow. People say I'm past my prime, (*Glances at Marianne*) for dancing that is. I remember you, you used to be a good dancer. How come you quit?

MARIANNE:

My life got stuck. So where are you off to next?

NOBLE:

First thing tomorrow, there's a convoy boogeying its way down to Michigan. Wanna come?

MARIANNE:

I already have a man, so to speak.

NOBLE:

Will he be in Michigan?

MARIANNE:

No.

NOBLE:

So what's your problem?

MARIANNE:

It's not that easy.

NOBLE:

But I am.

Noble grabs Marianne's hand and quickly leads her off stage. She laughs in surprise and delight.

SCENE 5

Angie and Andrew, in love but trying to hide it, are walking down a street, talking.

ANDREW:

So why'd you move here in the first place?

ANGIE:

Curiosity—about this side of my life. So voilà, here I am in pick-up truck city. Boy I hate country music.

ANDREW:

I love it.

ANGIE:

How can you love music about falling off bar stools and (*In a twang*) cheatin' on your woman?

ANDREW:

You've got a lot to learn about reserve life, Angie White.

ANGIE:

Tell me about it. I've been here all day watching the dancers strutting their stuff. Only I'm not quite sure what stuff it is that they're strutting. They don't show this kind of dancing on "Much Music." I don't know anything about this stuff—I wouldn't know a snake dance if it bit me. And a round dance, what the hell is that?

ANDREW:

(*Teasing*) That's when everybody who's around dances.

ANGIE:

Oh, and why do the drummers drum on the ground?

ANDREW:

Because they can't fly.

ANGIE:

You're making fun of me. Quit it. It's hard enough around here without you teasing me.

ANDREW:

Listen, I'll give you some advice. The entire philosophy of this whole reserve can be boiled down into three letters of the alphabet, B.L.T.

ANGIE:

B.L.T.?

ANDREW:

Bingo, liquor, and tournaments.

Uttering a brief scream, Angie darts into Andrew's arms.

ANDREW:

It's only a snake.

ANGIE:

I know that. I watched "Wild Kingdom." I just hate these bush things. They scare me to death. And all the noises, you should see me at night sometime. I'm walking down the roads and I'll hear a bush rustle or a tree creak. Bang, I'm in the nearest doorway so fast I'd run over rabbits.

ANDREW:

I noticed your legs. Well, here's your house. I used to play in your backyard when I was young.

ANGIE:

I bet you'd still like to.

ANDREW:

Uh, so do you want to get together later and do something? The reserve doesn't have to be as boring as you may think.

ANGIE:

Sounds great. (*Pause*) Oh I can't, not tonight. My mother has some friends staying over from the powwow. I have to hang around, cook, entertain, all that sort of stuff.

ANDREW:

No way of getting out of it?

ANGIE:

Can't. Promised my mom.

ANDREW:
Later?

ANGIE:
Sorry.

ANDREW:
When?

ANGIE:
Tomorrow?

ANDREW:
Tomorrow?!

ANGIE:
Yep.

ANDREW:
Okay.

ANGIE:
When?

ANDREW:
Breakfast?

ANGIE:
Yum.

ANDREW:
Tomorrow.

ANGIE:
Bye.

ANDREW:
Bye.

*They walk backwards a bit, not wanting to go.
Then they turn to leave.*

ANDREW:
And it's not even my birthday.

ANGIE:
And suddenly it's Christmas.

He walks off singing "Angie" by the Rolling Stones.

SCENE 6

Martha walks into the kitchen in her house. The kitchen is quite homey and clean, a kitchen a mother could be proud of (and she is). On the table is a bunch of receipts along with a cash box. Martha storms across the room, obviously not too happy. She sits down at the table and looks through all the bills and receipts.

MARTHA:

That'll teach me! Yep, it surely will. Never again will I use the Devil's tools to profit the Lord. (*Sadly*) I'll even give up bingo.

Andrew comes in the room loudly announcing his presence.

ANDREW:

What's on the stove, Mom? I'm hungry enough to eat a Mohawk, funny haircut and all.

MARTHA:

Oh behave you, I brought some food home from the Center. Mudbin. [Sit down.] Fix yourself something.

Andrew grabs a sandwich from a box on the table.

ANDREW:

Thanks Mom, worked up quite the appetite.

MARTHA:

Doing what?

ANDREW:

Walking with Angie. Angie White

MARTHA:

That's nice. Cousins should get to know each other.

ANDREW:

Cousins!! We're cousins?!

MARTHA:

Uh huh.

ANDREW:

You sure?

MARTHA:

Oh yes, you see my uncle on my mother's side used to be married to a certain Wilhimena George before she went crazy and tried to eat her cat. They had a child, I believe his name was Celestin. He was well known for his fondness for ladies and he ended up fathering a child out of wedlock with a young lady named Clyde.

ANDREW:

Clyde?!

MARTHA:

Her father had a peculiar sense of humor. Anyways, they didn't last long and if I remember correctly, Angie had a great-cousin, I think on her father's side, named Ben but everybody called him Boney, because the man was a living rack of bones. You could play "Amazing Grace" on his ribs. Come to think of it, Boney was also related to Angie's mother, twice removed from her grandfather's cousin. So these two met, Boney and Clyde, and god forbid if they didn't raise a whole batch of kids, one of whom was James.

ANDREW:

Wait a minute, wait a minute, that was Angie's father?

MARTHA:

He was no relation. Pay attention, Blue. He was adopted by Boney and Clyde cause his family couldn't take care of him. Now this was your father's cousin. So James ended up staying with Boney and Clyde and he eventually fell in love with Maggie and married her. Now Maggie is the aunt of Angie. See? Simple.

ANDREW:

(*Rubbing his temples*) We got any Tylenol?

MARTHA:

Bathroom, top shelf in the mirror.

ANDREW:

(*Dejected*) Cousins.

MARTHA:

Of course that's just the short version of the story.

ANDREW:

Oh well, it's back to the magazines.

MARTHA:

Pardon?

ANDREW:

Nothing, just a dream going up in smoke.

MARTHA:

That's nice, dear.

There's a knock at the door.

MARTHA:

Biingen. [Come in.]

David enters looking upset but perfectly dapper, as usual, in his designer jogging outfit.

DAVID:

(*Breathing deeply*) Martha ...

MARTHA:
That's a very nice outfit, David. You always look so good.

DAVID:
It's my new jogging outfit. I bought one for Marianne too, if I can ever find her. I want her to try it on before I remove the tags. You see, Martha, image is everything. That daughter of yours doesn't seem to understand that. Nor does she realize the effects her emotional problems toward machines will have on my relationship with the band manager.

Marianne enters the room, almost floating in.

MARIANNE:
Hello everybody.

DAVID:
Do you mind telling me where you've been all this time? Huh? Do you?

MARIANNE:
Oh David, you're here. Nice outfit. Let me guess, you got me one too?

DAVID:
Can you guess where I've just been?

MARIANNE:
(*Looks at David's suit*) The circus?

DAVID:
The community center, Marianne. And do you know what I found there?

MARIANNE:
A dead body draped over the stove, with a knife deep in its back, and a cryptic message scrawled in blood.

DAVID:

A broken typewriter. The *band's* broken typewriter.

MARIANNE:

Maybe the dead guy was holding it when he was stabbed.

DAVID:

You, Marianne, will be the death of me yet.

ANDREW:

Lighten up, David, nobody dies from a broken typewriter.

DAVID:

They do when it's band property. Remember what happened to Fabian last year?

MARIANNE:

But that's different. You just don't decide to party in a cement mixer. That's stupid.

ANDREW:

He did end up as a damn good war memorial though. Where were you anyways?

Martha slaps his arm urging him to be quiet and inconspicuous.

MARTHA:

Bzaanyaan. [Be quiet.]

DAVID:

Marianne, I think you need professional help. The band manager …

MARIANNE:

Professional help?! Hell, David, you need some serious partying help. Try singing a song or doing a dance once, you might like it. Do you know what your problem is, David? You need to live on the wild side for a while. Go crazy, put the pedal to the metal, go skinny dipping, try seeing a movie without reading two reviews first, or even, if you dare, try calling the band manager Frankie.

DAVID:
I did. Once.

MARIANNE:
When?

DAVID:
Remember last February when I got sent to Moose Factory for three weeks? Just before then.

Marianne and Andrew laugh.

DAVID:
That's enough of this. Marianne Elizabeth, I demand to know who you were with.

MARIANNE:
I went for a drive.

DAVID:
But I had the car.

MARIANNE:
(*Dreamily*) Other people drive cars too, you know. Cars with balls, that still have a speedometer in miles, and seats that go down.

DAVID:
Do these people have names?

MARIANNE:
A friend named Noble.

DAVID:
Noble?! What kind of name is Noble?

MARIANNE:
He told me it's short for Noble Savage.

DAVID:
Noble Savage! How amusing. It's time to go home now, Marianne. I've invited the band manager over for dinner to better explain your problem with machines.

MARIANNE:
>Maybe I don't wanna go home.

DAVID:
>(*Wearily*) Now Marianne …

MARIANNE:
>Maybe I want to spend some time with my little brother.

>*She grabs and hugs Andrew, almost smothering and crushing him.*

MARIANNE:
>Maybe I want to stay here with my family, people I love and respect.

DAVID:
>No, Marianne!

MARIANNE:
>Yes, David. Read my lips. Yes meaning I'm not going home with you, but yes I'm staying here. Try and move me.

>*She glares defiantly into David's eyes.*

DAVID:
>You want to stay here? Fine, then stay here. Maybe I should cook anyways. The band manager is allergic to Klik.

>*David slams his fist on the table as he leaves. He is halfway across the floor before he stops.*

DAVID:
>Sorry about hitting your table, Martha.

MARTHA:
>No problem, David.

>*David leaves.*

MARTHA:
>What in God's great mercy is the matter with you two?

MARIANNE:

Oh it's David. He's going through one of his jerk phases. It happens occasionally. Women have periods, men have jerk phases.

ANDREW:

I hope this car ride of yours was worth it.

MARIANNE:

It was like reliving a dream. A girl's allowed to dream, isn't she, Mom?

MARTHA:

Oh don't be silly, I haven't dreamed in 40 years, and I'm just jim dandy.

ANDREW:

Who's Jim Dandy?

MARTHA:

And don't start up with me either, I've got too many things on my mind right now to bother with you two.

ANDREW:

Problems, Mom?

MARTHA:

Now don't you worry about that. You just go settle down and get used to your home again.

ANDREW:

Okay, you're the boss.

He starts moving toward his room.

MARIANNE:

Maybe me and Blue can help?

MARTHA:

I'll figure this out myself.

As Andrew approaches his room, atmosphere music slowly comes up. It should have the same feel as "Chariots Of Fire" or "2001: A Space Odyssey." The room is suddenly flooded with light revealing an awesome sight to Andrew. An entire wall of his bedroom is covered with 143 cases of beer, stacked in neat rows. He shakes his head to clear it and looks again. He runs to it in slow motion. He reaches out gingerly and touches one of the cases to see if it's really there. He looks to the heavens.

ANDREW:

Thank you! They're all here, all of them.

Andrew shakes a case of Canadian, creating the telltale sound of bottles rattling.

ANDREW:

The national anthem!!

He reaches out to grab one when he hears his mother's voice.

MARTHA:

Blue! Don't you dare touch that beer. Your room is the only place I could find to store it. It belongs to the committee.

Crestfallen, Andrew looks back upwards.

ANDREW:

(Disgusted) Thanks. I'll never be able to sleep

Back in the kitchen, Marianne sits down beside Martha.

MARIANNE:

So that's where you put it. I told you if you wanted you could store the stuff at my place.

MARTHA:

Iizan-gonaa! [As if!]

Andrew walks in, looking stunned.

MARTHA:
> Blue, are you all right?

ANDREW:
> There must be over 100 cases of beer in there.

MARTHA:
> One hundred and forty-three to be exact. (*She bursts into tears*) And it's all that crazy old Marjorie's fault. I bet she did this all so she could become president of the committee. They're gonna burn me at the stake and Marjorie will be buying the gasoline.

MARIANNE:
> How much have you sold already?

MARTHA:
> Twenty-two.

MARIANNE:
> (*Shocked*) Only 22 cases?!

MARTHA:
> Twenty-two bottles! (*She starts crying again*) Not even a full case. And every last one of them was bought by Crazy Fiddler, bless his beer-soaked little heart. I'm doomed, doomed.

MARIANNE:
> Well, what do you think we should do?

ANDREW:
> Get our skates.

MARIANNE:
> What?

ANDREW:
> Hell has got to be freezing over.

SCENE 7

It's nighttime and David is jogging with a walk-man. He stops to rest. Suddenly Noble appears from behind.

NOBLE:

Yo, bro. (*David doesn't hear*) Yo, bro.

He leans over and taps David on the shoulder.

DAVID:

Ahhhhh!

NOBLE:

Sorry about the scare, guy. You got a light?

DAVID:

Hardly.

NOBLE:

Too bad. Nice outfit. Where'd you get it? Goofs-Are-Us? Christ, I'd be running too if I wore an outfit like that on my reserve.

DAVID:

It's a jogging outfit.

NOBLE:

It's a goof outfit. Hey man, sorry, I didn't mean to make fun of your outfit. Actually I did but sorry anyways.

DAVID:

What are you doing here? I thought the pow-wow was over.

NOBLE:

The pow's gone so now we're trying for the wow. There's a party down by the camping area. You wanna come to the party? Goof suit and all.

DAVID:

No thank you, but perhaps you can help me. Would you happen to know a gentleman by the name of Noble?

Noble is startled but defensive.

NOBLE:
Nope, never met the man. But whatever he did, I'm sure it was an accident. Gotta be going. Bye.

DAVID:
Wait a minute. (*Pause*) You look like a Noble Savage.

NOBLE:
Why, thank you. I think.

DAVID:
Yeah, you look like the scraggly type she used to hang around with a long time ago. You're this Noble guy, aren't you?

NOBLE:
She? What she?

DAVID:
Marianne.

NOBLE:
You're David? (*Looks David up and down*) She was right.

DAVID:
What did you and Marianne do this afternoon?

NOBLE:
Talk about déjà vu.

DAVID:
Talk about Marianne.

NOBLE:
No.

They stare at each other, a Mexican standoff.

SCENE 8

Marianne and Andrew are sitting in his bedroom. It's nighttime. They are sitting on the bed staring longingly at the beer.

ANDREW/MARIANNE:

(*Singing*) A hundred forty-three cases of beer on the wall, a hundred forty-three cases of beer …

MARIANNE:

(*Singing*) You take one down, you pass it around …

ANDREW:

Don't even think it!!

MARIANNE:

Come on, Blue. There are 143 cases here, she won't miss one.

ANDREW:

No! I will not be involved in any of your little schemes. You used to always get me in trouble when we were kids. I'm still in the record books as the youngest child ever to be fined by the police. You're 10 years older than me, you should know better.

MARIANNE:

It was just a suggestion.

ANDREW:

Besides, Mom told me she took a polaroid of this wall, she knows where every beer is.

MARIANNE:

She doesn't trust us?

ANDREW:

Marianne, when you were 17 you tried to sell our house for prom money, remember?

MARIANNE:

That was a long time ago.

ANDREW:

And you didn't even have a date.

MARIANNE:

Okay, okay, I get the point.

There's a gentle knocking on the door. It's Martha.

ANDREW:

Mom, you still up?

Martha enters in her nightgown and cap, looking very matronly. She appears worried and sits down. Now all three are looking at the beer.

MARTHA:

I can't sleep. This beer is keeping me up.

MARIANNE:

That's funny. It usually puts me to sleep.

MARTHA:

I've tried to lead a good life, really I have. And this is my thanks. Maybe I should just pack up and move to one of them far-off places like Tahiti.

ANDREW:

Mom, you wouldn't like it down there. No bingo. And I think they're all Protestant.

MARTHA:

Never mind. But I have to do something.

ANDREW:

Why don't you just take the beer back? You have a permit, don't you?

MARTHA:

Of course I have a permit. I'm a law-abiding citizen. That Marjorie filled it out for me. She and that smart-as-a-dead chicken son of hers picked up the beer too. That's where it all started. The two of them took all the stickers off the cases. There's such a thing as being too neat.

ANDREW:
Stickers?

MARIANNE:
Little yellow stickers you need on the case to take it back. No sticker, no returned money.

MARTHA:
I don't believe that woman had the patience to pick off 143 stickers cause they didn't look right. That woman boggles my mind.

ANDREW:
Hey Marianne, how about this? Why don't you bootleg it, Mom?

MARTHA:
What?

MARIANNE:
(*Laughing*) What an idea! Yeah Mom, you could make all your money back for sure and a bit of profit. All the other bootleggers are probably dry after this weekend anyways.

MARTHA:
Bootlegging?

Andrew and Marianne are having a great time joking, but Martha has a serious look on her face. Suddenly there's a knock that turns into pounding at the front door.

MARTHA:
Who could that be at this hour?

MARIANNE:
I'll get it.

ANDREW:
Mom, we'd have to get you a pager like Old Man Johnson.

MARIANNE:

(*As she's leaving*) And an answering machine.

ANDREW:

For sure. Just think, Mom, you could have all that beer gone, a fortune in money, and the committee will love you. Mom! Bootlegging!

They both laugh, Marianne from the kitchen. The pounding gets louder, annoying Marianne.

MARIANNE:

Hold your horses or I'll shove them down your throat.

Andrew is still chuckling to himself, unaware of Martha's deep thought.

MARTHA:

Hmmm, bootlegging.

Marianne opens the door to find Noble, completely drunk.

MARIANNE:

Noble? What are you doing here? Do you know what time it is?

NOBLE:

(*Smiling*) Goof alert. Goof alert.

He falls forward, passed out, onto the floor.

The lights go down.

END OF ACT I

ACT II

SCENE I

Angie is standing in Martha's kitchen. It is early morning and she has a cup of coffee in her hand. The noise of hammering can be heard coming from just outside the house. Off in the corner is a guitar case. On the table is an open bag of potato chips.

ANGIE:
So beautiful out there, (*Looks toward Andrew's bedroom*) so beautiful in there. So close, yet so far.

Marianne's booming voice can suddenly be heard.

MARIANNE:
Answer the door. (*The hammering continues*) I said answer the door.

Marianne lumbers into sight, and groggily goes toward the door.

ANGIE:
That was hammering.

MARIANNE:
Hammering?

ANGIE:
Yeah, Sleeping Beauty.

MARIANNE:
(*Crossly*) Die.

Marianne lumbers over to the coffee machine and fills two cups.

ANGIE:
No thanks, I have some.

MARIANNE:
Who cares? Why are you here anyways?

ANGIE:
I'm here for breakfast.

Andrew walks on stage to the refrigerator, also half-asleep. He is dressed only in his camouflage-colored underwear. Without noticing Angie or Marianne, he drinks from a carton of milk. Angie watches him with an appreciative eye.

ANGIE:
Nice camouflage, what are you trying to hide?

Andrew is startled. He looks at Angie, then at his near nudity. He tries to cover himself with a dish towel.

ANDREW:
What are you doing here?

ANGIE:
Having a cup of coffee and ...

Angie grabs the dish towel.

ANGIE:
... enjoying the view.

ANDREW:
Hey, give that back!

They end up having a tug of war with the dish towel. Marianne barely notices, more intent on staring into her two cups of coffee.

ANGIE:
Come on, don't be bashful, soldier, show me your weapons.

ANDREW:
I don't show my weapons to relative strangers.

ANGIE:
Well, who do you show them to?

ANDREW:
You're missing the point, cousin.

ANGIE:

Cousin?!

Andrew makes a run for his bedroom.

ANDREW:

(*Yelling*) Yeah, cousin.

ANGIE:

Marianne, I have a problem.

MARIANNE:

You're 22, single, and thin. Unless you've gotten something terminal, I don't want to hear it.

Angie casts a longing look in Andrew's direction.

ANGIE:

What a waste.

MARIANNE:

You got the hots for him or something?

ANGIE:

It shows?

MARIANNE:

Any more obvious and I'd be hosing you down.

ANGIE:

Everybody I meet on this stupid reserve is my cousin.

MARIANNE:

What's your problem?

ANGIE:

Well for one thing, he isn't six foot four. Hell, I'm almost as tall as him, and you've got bigger biceps. And I sure as hell can't find out about the rest of him now. I had my future husband pegged as some tall blond god with more money than brains. What have I got? A pint-sized Dick Tracy, not even a real cop, a *special constable*. What's a special constable you may ask? I have no idea, I think that means they can shoot unarmed ducks.

MARIANNE:

Well, a real cop arrests people, then has a donut. A special constable warns people, then has bannock.

ANGIE:

And the thing that really pisses me off, and I do mean royally, is the only Indian I've ever been attracted to, and lord knows I've been hit on by quite a few, happens to be my cousin.

MARIANNE:

Did I doze off? I thought you liked my brother?

ANGIE:

I could just die.

MARIANNE:

Don't tell me it's Michael at the clinic? That man would bang a moose if he was taller.

ANGIE:

(*Confused*) What?

MARIANNE:

Listen, for the last 10 years I've been living with a man whose idea of foreplay is stroking the band council. What do I have to show for it? A brand new Volkswagen Passat with every conceivable option in the universe. Three bathrooms— there are only two of us—go figure it. And a satellite dish that brings in 416 stations worldwide. Who cares about the top 10 shows in Bulgaria? I got everything I ever wanted ... except the David I fell in love with.

ANGIE:

Well, David does try to help you. He's always concerned about what you do and where you are, that must count for something? And didn't he put the two of you on a diet?

MARIANNE:

Have a potato chip. Angie, don't make the same mistakes I did.

ANGIE:

I haven't had a date in five months. I don't need this kind of advice.

MARIANNE:

You remind me so much of myself when I was your age.

ANGIE:

(*Concerned*) What happened?

MARIANNE:

I thought it was time to settle down. If I settle down any further I'll be in China.

ANGIE:

Oh Marianne, you're still young, sort of. Maybe all David needs is a good kick in the behind. We all need that sometimes.

MARIANNE:

Oh I've thought of kicking him, not in the behind, mind you. Men! God must have one hell of a sense of humor. Anyways, what was all that about cousins? I was sort of fuzzy in the middle.

ANGIE:

Didn't you hear him? Andrew is my cousin!

MARIANNE:

Of for the love of … Yes you're cousins, cousins by marriage. You see, my uncle on my grand-mother's side used to be married to …

ANGIE:

By marriage? That makes it okay?

MARIANNE:

Yeah yeah, what are you waiting for? Sic'em.

Marianne points to Andrew's room.

MARIANNE:
> Just listen for him mumbling something about room numbers I think. All night it was 34B and 34C.

> *Angie goes to his door and knocks gently.*

ANGIE:
> Hello, Blue.

ANDREW:
> There's no one in here but us cousins.

> *Angie slowly opens the door and enters Andrew's bedroom. Andrew is getting dressed.*

ANGIE:
> (*Noticing the beer*) Wha?!

ANDREW:
> Good choice of words.

> *Angie looks at the beer, then at Andrew, then back to the beer.*

ANGIE:
> Decisions, decisions.

> *Andrew notices her eyeing the beer.*

ANDREW:
> Uh uh.

ANGIE:
> No?

ANDREW:
> My mother gently warned me not to touch the beer or I won't be able to have any children.

ANGIE:
> Aren't you a pretty sight in the morning?

ANDREW:
> I didn't sleep well.

ANGIE:
> Why didn't you try counting sheep?

ANDREW:

I tried that. But after the first few sheep jump over that stupid fence, they start turning into beer cases. Then I see hundreds of beer cases jumping over that same fence, all crying "beeeer, beeeer, beeeer."

ANGIE:

I'll say this, it sure does look good and appetizing.

Andrew's eyes wander over Angie.

ANDREW:

You can say that again.

ANGIE:

And you can't touch it.

ANDREW:

I know.

ANGIE:

I bet you'd love to just dive right in.

Andrew is practically drooling.

ANDREW:

Is it getting hot in here or something?

Angie moves in toward him slowly, her purpose clear. She puts a hand softly on his cheek and draws him toward her.

ANDREW:

Angie, we're related!

ANGIE:

By marriage.

ANDREW:

Marriage?

ANGIE:

Uh huh.

ANDREW:

That means ...

ANGIE:

Uh huh. And your mother probably won't be home for quite some time.

ANDREW:

Mom always was good to me.

Marianne is in the kitchen lazily chomping on potato chips. David is at the door watching her. He's soaking wet and dirty.

DAVID:

How about some breakfast?

Marianne holds up the potato chips.

MARIANNE:

Pretend these are homefries.

DAVID:

I remember when we used to have nice big breakfasts. Eggs, bacon, sausages, potatoes, toast. Whatever happened to them?

MARIANNE:

Hey, you wanna be Mr. Fitness or you want a button-popping breakfast?

DAVID:

I want both.

MARIANNE:

You can't have both.

DAVID:

Maybe I'd just like to try and break even.

MARIANNE:

There's more to life than breaking even. (*Pause*) I'm leaving you, David.

DAVID:

Oh.

MARIANNE:

I was wondering how you'd take it.

DAVID:

No reason why I should rant and rave.

MARIANNE:

I used to like that in you, the way you could rationalize everything. Other people would be arguing and carrying on, but not you. You'd be telling me about some new things you learned in school. It was sort of an anchor for me, back in my wilder days. But it wasn't an anchor, it was a mooring post. If you're tied up all the time, you never get to go anywhere. Well, this girl is out of the marina.

She gets up, ready to face the music and her decision. Then she sees David fully for the first time.

MARIANNE:

What happened? You look terrible. Calvin Klein die? My god, David, you're wet!

DAVID:

Thank you, I missed that. I met Mr. Noble last night.

MARIANNE:

David, I really don't want to … (*She sees something outside*) David? Whose car is that in the driveway?

DAVID:

Ours.

MARIANNE:

I can see the trail of mud from the car to the door. Where's our Passat?

DAVID:

Answer me this, Marianne. Are you planning to run off with this unemployed feather jumper and leave me here after 10 years? Yesterday I might have laid right down and let you walk all over me, but not today. Your behavior is outrageous, unacceptable, and I demand an explanation.

MARIANNE:
Would you like a type-written report?

DAVID:
We can't afford another typewriter.

MARIANNE:
You're such a clerk!

DAVID:
I am not a clerk.

MARIANNE:
Yes you are, and so am I. Oh David, between the two of us we push more paper than lumberjacks.

DAVID:
Oh, living out of a van is better?

MARIANNE:
Maybe not better but it's a living.

DAVID:
Is he still here? Your Noble Savage is hiding here somewhere, isn't he? Drag him out this moment. Come on, Marianne, I know he's in this house.

MARIANNE:
Oh forget about it, David. Noble was just a flash from the past. The man is long gone. History.

A groan is heard, and Noble stumbles into view, suffering from the hangover from hell.

DAVID:
History repeats itself.

NOBLE:
Where do I pay my fine?

MARIANNE:
(*To Noble*) Why aren't you gone yet? (*To David*) He showed up last night drunk. We put him in the spare bedroom to sleep it off. He said he'd be long gone by dawn on a convoy to Michigan. Honest! Why aren't you gone yet?

NOBLE:
I'm history. Which way is north?

DAVID:
That way.

MARIANNE:
You still look a little rough.

NOBLE:
Which way?

DAVID:
That way.

MARIANNE:
But there's no road in that direction, just bush.

NOBLE:
How about east?

MARIANNE:
David, he's in no shape to travel.

Noble starts to feel sick.

NOBLE:
(*Looking around*) The can?

DAVID/MARIANNE:
(*Quickly*) West.

Noble shuffles toward the bathroom.

Back in his bedroom, Andrew sits up, alarmed.

ANDREW:
She's doing what?!

They jump out of bed.

NOBLE:
(*Leans against a wall for support*)
Whoa ... how'd you get this rippling effect?

MARIANNE:
Yo, Weekend Warrior, could you use some nice
fried eggs?

This is too much for Noble's delicate condition. He races for the bathroom as she begins frying eggs. Andrew and Angie run past Noble causing him to spin.

ANGIE:
Hey, it's nice buns.

ANDREW:
Emergency. (*To Angie*) Go ahead, tell her.

ANGIE:
Tell her what?

ANDREW:
The signs.

ANGIE:
Oh. Your mother is putting signs up all over the reserve offering to sell beer to people.

Noble sticks his head out of the bathroom, hearing the magic words.

NOBLE:
There's beer here?

David threatens Noble, who disappears again.

ANDREW:
Out of this house. With this phone number. This unlisted phone number.

MARIANNE:
Mom?!

Marianne starts laughing at the absurdity of it all.

DAVID:
Martha is selling beer?

ANDREW:
Bootlegging.

DAVID:
Oh my god, no.

ANDREW:

(*To Marianne*) Will you snap out of it.

DAVID:

I wondered about the sign out front. I just glanced at it. I thought it was for a rummage sale.

ANDREW:

Marianne! I'm in law enforcement. I can't have Mother bootlegging.

Angie notices the water on the floor from David's soaked clothes.

ANGIE:

Why is the floor wet?

ANDREW:

Marianne! Are you going to help or not?

Marianne is still laughing.

DAVID:

(*To Angie*) You don't want to know.

ANDREW:

Fine then. I'll do it myself. As a soon-to-be special constable I will take the law into my own hands and do my best to save our asses. Angie, let's go.

ANGIE:

Where are we going?

Andrew drags her out the door.

ANDREW:

To find all those damn signs before the real cops find them.

The phone rings and David answers it.

DAVID:

Hello. (*Pause*) No, she's not here, can I take a message? (*Pause*) Pardon. (*Pause*) I don't quite understand. Are you sure you don't want Citizenship Canada, if you want to know about Canadians? (*Pause*) Oh, you want to buy some Canadian. I suppose I can take an order. Okay, I'll tell her.

Noble stumbles out. He's got a wet towel wrapped around his head.

NOBLE:

Eggs?

David hangs up and looks at the message.

DAVID:

This can't be happening.

Noble sneaks a peek through his towel at Marianne.

NOBLE:

Who are you? (*He remembers*) Oh yeah. (*Looks at David*) Hey, recall! Sorry about your car, man. No hard feelings.

MARIANNE:

What about our car?

DAVID:

You'll burn the eggs.

NOBLE:

You should have seen it. Man oh man! Most amazing thing I have ever seen, and I've seen a few. That Passat car of yours sailed out a good 40 feet or so.

MARIANNE:

The Passat! You crashed our Passat?!

NOBLE:

The water sort of cushioned the landing.

MARIANNE:
Water?!

NOBLE:
What was the name of that place again?

DAVID:
Mud Lake.

MARIANNE:
Our Volkswagen Passat is at the bottom of Mud Lake?

DAVID:
Not any more.

MARIANNE:
We haven't finished paying for it yet, David!

DAVID:
We went and called a tow truck immediately.

The telephone rings.

DAVID:
I'll get that.

David answers the phone, and writes down a beer order as the dialogue continues.

NOBLE:
You shoulda been there, man. Electrical system is shot all to hell and gone. Baby! The way all the lights went off and on under the water. Actually it was kind of pretty. Blink blink. Blink blink. Blink blink.

MARIANNE:
Blink, blink?!

NOBLE:
And there was old David, bobbing to the surface.

David hangs up the phone.

MARIANNE:
David, tell me no one saw you. David!

NOBLE:

Are you kidding? When everybody heard about it we just shifted the party to the lake. One of the best, Dave, one of the best. But we ran out of beer and that's how I got here. Some old gal named Marjorie sent me up here looking for more.

MARIANNE:

How, in God's name, did all this start?

NOBLE:

Well, sweetheart, we was having a drag race and lover boy there forgot to hit the brakes.

MARIANNE:

(*To David*) You idiot! David, you?

DAVID:

You're the one that told me to go out and party.

MARIANNE:

David …

DAVID:

And that's not the worst of it. My briefcase with all my papers in it for this week's council meeting … is now swimming upstream.

MARIANNE:

Talk about polluting the water. On second thought, just don't bother talking to me at all. Ever again.

NOBLE:

Excuse me, the food. Got any toast?

The phone rings, David quickly answers and begins taking a message. Marianne starts cooking again.

DAVID:

Hello. (*Pause*) Oh hi, Aunt Vanessa, Martha's not here right now. (*Pause*) A case? But you don't drink. (*Pause*) Aunt Vanessa, I know Erica's getting married next week, but when they say "something borrowed, something blue," I don't think they meant a case of Blue Light. (*Pause*) Fine, Aunt Vanessa. Goodbye.

David hangs up. Marianne slaps a plateful of eggs in front of Noble and David.

MARIANNE:

Eggs.

DAVID:

Not that greasy stuff.

Noble grabs David's plate and lets David's eggs fall onto his plate. Martha walks in the door with a very satisfied smile on her face. She stops and looks at the wet floor.

MARTHA:

Who's been mopping? (*Looks at Noble*) I see you've decided to join the living.

Noble says something but is unintelligible because his mouth is full of food.

MARTHA:

I've got signs and flyers all across the village. They always say it pays to advertise. Look at this. (*Holds up some paper*) Thirty-five orders in the last half-hour. A miracle. I'm thinking of putting something out in the church bulletin.

The phone rings again. Martha, excited, goes to answer it.

MARTHA:

My first call!

DAVID:

Actually …

MARTHA:

(*On the phone*) Ahneen, Lester. (*Pause*) No. (*Pause*) No! I will not sell you any beer, Lester. You're my brother and one of my rules is I refuse to sell to any of my brothers. (*Pause*) Eddie don't count, with a wife like that, he needs a beer. (*Pause*) I know. (*Pause*) I know. (*Pause*) I know, Lester. (*Pause*) No. (*She hangs up*) I swear that man would try to sweet-talk the devil out of his pitchfork.

NOBLE:
You've got beer here?

DAVID:
Martha! What has gone wrong with you? You're 58 years old.

MARTHA:
I'm 58 years young!

DAVID:
You're almost a senior citizen.

MARTHA:
Prove it.

DAVID:
You belong with the Church Recreation Committee. You're supposed to knit and make soup. Not bootleg!

MARTHA:
David? You're soggy.

NOBLE:
Excuse me. The beer. How much?

DAVID:
(*Still pushing*) Martha, the police ...

MARTHA:
... won't bother me. They're such wonderful boys. Did you know I used to babysit one of them years ago? Used to be kind of sweet on Marianne till she handcuffed him to a cow.

DAVID:
But Martha, you can't just ... (*Turns to Marianne*) You handcuffed a cop to a cow?
(*She shrugs, his attention turns back to Martha*) They're not just going to turn the other way.

NOBLE:
Do you take checks?

The phone rings again and Martha gets it.

MARTHA:

(*Answering*) Ahneen. (*Pause*) Scarecrow Jones, how long has it been? (*Pause*) That long, huh? (*Pause*) Off on good behavior. I'm so happy for you. What can I do for you? (*Pause*) Only one case, Scarecrow, that doesn't sound like you. (*Pause*) I see, you're getting off the road but not quite on the wagon. I'll see what I can do.

She hangs up the phone and David is stunned.

DAVID:

You're bootlegging to ex-cons?!

MARTHA:

Oh, Scarecrow's a nice ex-con. It wasn't his fault he went to jail. The courts overreacted.

DAVID:

What did he do?

MARTHA:

One night he went to the zoo and let some of the animals out.

DAVID:

That doesn't sound so bad.

MARTHA:

Of course he shot three of them, took them home, and ate them.

DAVID:

I don't believe this.

MARTHA:

That's what gave him the idea to open the restaurant.

NOBLE:

Goddamn it, I said I'll buy some beer.

Martha gives Noble a good swat to the head.

MARTHA:

(*To David*) It's nice to see you and Marianne together again.

DAVID:

I wouldn't be too sure about that. Your daughter seems to have some other ideas.

MARIANNE:

Like maybe I want to see the world before I see 40.

MARTHA:

I'm about to see 60 and I know the world is in here, (*Pats her heart*) not out there.

The phone rings again and Martha eagerly answers it.

MARTHA:

Ahneen. (*Her voice becomes tight*) Well hello there, Marjorie. How nice of you to call. What can I do for you?

DAVID:

I can't believe you're serious about leaving me for that.

Noble burps.

MARTHA:

No, I've given up bingo. I haven't got the time since you saddled me up with 143 cases of beer. It seems like I've devoted my life to looking after those beer. Pretty soon I'll be giving them names. (*Pause*) No Marjorie, I will not listen to any more of your foolish fund-raising ideas. (*Pause*) A what? For god's sake woman, nobody in this village would pay good money to see your son as the first Indian Elvis impersonator. Now are you gonna order some-thing or not? (*Pause*) Fine. Thanks for supporting the church, Marjorie.

She hangs up the phone angrily.

MARTHA:

That woman is more bother than she's worth. Marianne, are you and David staying for dinner?

MARIANNE:

Um …

MARTHA:

We're having pot roast tonight with garden fresh beans from our garden. Marianne honey, will you go pick some beans for dinner?

MARIANNE:

This one last time, Mother.

David watches her exit until Martha gives him a shove.

MARTHA:

Don't just stand there, go talk to her. Why do you think I sent her out there?

DAVID:

For beans?

MARTHA:

I hate beans.

DAVID:

Ohhhh!

David exits.

MARTHA:

In my day, relationships were held together with twine and bailing wire, today it's scotch tape and staples.

Martha turns to Noble.

MARTHA:

What's your name again, boy?

NOBLE:

Noble.

MARTHA:

And what do you do?

NOBLE:
> Depends what I can get away with. I'm kidding.
> I'm a dancer during the summer, and I do all
> sorts of odd jobs in the winter.

MARTHA:
> That's it?

NOBLE:
> That's enough. I have a good time, make a living.
> Someday I'll be rich though, I saw it in a dream.

MARTHA:
> Oh yeah, how?

NOBLE:
> Don't know. The truck hit a bump and I woke up.
>
> *Again Martha doesn't laugh. Noble isn't charming her
> as he expected to.*

MARTHA:
> Do you go to church?

NOBLE:
> My parents used to take me as a kid but it wasn't
> for me. All that standing, sitting, kneeling, stand-
> ing, sitting, kneeling. Made me feel like a little
> brown yoyo.

MARTHA:
> You should go back to church.

NOBLE:
> I like to think that I do in a way. That's why I go
> to powwows. It's a chance to sleep under the
> stars, the light bulbs of Heaven, on the grass,
> listen to the trees and the insects. To me, that's
> the voice of the Creator. I'd rather hear the voice
> myself than go through a middle man.

MARTHA:
> Yet you drink.

NOBLE:

You smoke. So we're both a little naughty. Who isn't?

Martha studies him for a while, sizing him up. The next interchange is in Ojibway.

MARTHA:

Kiinwaa wezhkiniigjig noogom. [You young people of today.]

NOBLE:

Wagnen niinwind? [What about us?]

MARTHA:

Gdoo-nisitaw? Gdi-nishnaabem. [You understand me? You speak Indian.]

NOBLE:

Nagitsiimag ngii-kinoomaagoog. Pii-windendsigwaa namewgamig. [I learned it from my parents when they weren't in church.]

Martha smiles at Noble for the first time. They go back to English.

MARTHA:

You want to stay for dinner?

NOBLE:

That depends.

MARTHA:

On what?

NOBLE:

Who has to say grace?

Martha actually laughs and Noble smiles too. The phone rings as Andrew and Angie enter carrying painted signs and paper notices.

MARTHA:

My signs, Blue!

NOBLE:

>Far out, you named him after a beer. I had a cousin named after a beer. Boy, I haven't seen O.V. in years. I'll get the phone. (*He picks up the receiver*) And a howdy doody morning to you. Come to Martha's first if you have a thirst.

ANGIE:

>Where would you like these?

MARTHA:

>Back on the trees. I spent all morning putting those signs up. Why did you take them down?

ANDREW:

>Mother, there is an art to bootlegging. You don't just paint a four foot by four foot sign in big red letters saying "BEER FOR SALE: SEE MARTHA" and ram it into the ground beside the police station. I just spent the last 15 minutes convincing Constable Gale that I was in the process of having you committed. He sends his sympathies.

>*Noble puts the phone down and starts fiddling with a nearby guitar.*

MARTHA:

>What's wrong with what I'm doing?

ANDREW:

>Will someone talk sense to the woman!

MARTHA:

>I'll have you know, young man, I was talking sense long before you were born.

ANDREW:

>Mom, please! My buddies are leaning out of windows throwing orders for cases at me. It's ... humiliating!

MARTHA:

>You picked up more orders?

ANDREW:

What you're doing is immoral. You're contributing to the drinking problem in our village. Angie, say something.

ANGIE:

I don't think it's that immoral. She's not selling to anybody under 19, or anybody with children to feed. It says so on the signs. She's not encouraging people to drink, in fact the price of bootleg beer is enough to stop them from drinking. She's just selling it to people who would have bought it anyways. And since she delivers, nobody will be drinking and driving. And I can think of worse places for the money to go than the church. So what's wrong with that?

MARTHA:

Thank you.

ANDREW:

Whose side are you on?

ANGIE:

Sorry.

She goes into the living room where Noble is strumming a guitar.

ANDREW:

The bottom line is this is illegal, pure and simple. You do this, you're breaking the law.

MARTHA:

You sometimes drive 90 in an 80-kilometer zone. I've seen you do it, Blue. Isn't that breaking the law?

ANDREW:

I give up. A son is supposed to make life miserable for his mother, not the other way around.

Marianne and David enter from the garden.

MARIANNE:

I don't want to be an Indian yuppie. I want bannock, not whole wheat. I want to fry my food, not microwave it. Especially that quiche stuff of yours. The Creator meant eggs to be fried, not baked.

Angie takes the guitar and starts strumming.

DAVID:

I am simply trying to offer a healthy alternative to pop and chips.

MARIANNE:

I hate tofu, alfalfa sprouts, soya bean curd, and most of all, and I really mean this, David, I really hate skim milk.

DAVID:

And now I'm being attacked for showing my concern for you.

MARIANNE:

I appreciate your concern, but you're a bully, David.

DAVID:

I most certainly am not.

MARIANNE:

You make me eat all that stuff. You don't ask me, you tell me. Now I'm telling you.

MARTHA:

Did you get the beans?

MARIANNE:

Enjoy them.

The phone rings.

MARTHA:

Excuse me, David.

DAVID:

No problem, Martha.

MARTHA:

(*Answering the phone*) Ahneen. Young William, what can I do for you? (*Pause*) Three cases?! You should be ashamed of yourself, young man, spending money on all that beer. You've got three children in that household to look after. (*Pause*) I don't care if only one is yours. You behave or I'll report you to the police.

She hangs up angrily.

NOBLE:

You got a cool mother.

ANDREW:

My bootlegging mother.

Angie starts playing in earnest, and singing with Marianne and Noble joining in.

> She's got the blues
> That ain't no news
> She's got the blues
> 'Cause she's sellin' them two by two
> Talkin' 'bout the Bootlegger Blues
> She's got the blues
> That ain't no news
> We're talkin' 'bout the Bootlegger Blues
>
> Now she can make a cake
> Now she can shake 'n bake
> She can clean a house
> She might even mend a blouse
> But the one thing she can really do
> Is sell you some Blue
>
> Yeah, we're talkin' 'bout the Bootlegger Blues
>
> Oh we've got beer up the walls
> And sittin' in the halls
> Mom been on the phone
> Turnin' down a loan
> She stands at the sink

With her hands full of dishes
She's the only lady in the village
Who can make or break your wishes
We're talkin' 'bout you bootlegger you
Martha

The song ends with people breaking down in laughter except David and Martha.

MARTHA:
Oh you think it's so funny, do you? Well, laugh all you want as you deliver these.

ANDREW:
(*Takes the list*) You can't be serious. There must be 50 names here. And these are some of the scum of the village.

MARTHA:
Them are your cousins, now scoot.

ANDREW:
Mom, how am I gonna cart all this beer around? We don't have a car.

MARTHA:
You're young, carry it.

ANDREW:
Oh Mom …

ANGIE:
There must be another way.

All heads swivel to David.

MARTHA:
David …

DAVID:
Oh no you don't. Keep me and my car, and I use the term loosely, out of this. I am not in the mood to take part in any illegal activities.

MARTHA:
But David …

DAVID:

No buts. Sorry Martha, but being arrested for bootlegging would just about cap off my day.

ANGIE:

Come on, David, it won't take long.

DAVID:

Only 30 to 60 days. (*To Marianne*) And you keep out of this.

MARIANNE:

Noble's got wheels. I'm sure we can use his car.

NOBLE:

Sure, put as much in as you can. Fill it to the top.

DAVID:

The heck you will. This is family business. Martha, take the Camaro.

One by one they all peek out the window to look at his car.

ANDREW:

That's your car in the driveway? David, you won't even drive on the same side of the road as a Camaro.

DAVID:

It's a loaner from the towing company. (*Miserably*) A '75 Camaro.

ANGIE:

Well, should we start loading up?

ANDREW:

Where's the Passat?

MARIANNE:

Contrary to popular belief, Volkswagens cannot dogpaddle.

ANDREW:

Huh?

ANGIE:

Hey guys, who's for loading up?

MARTHA:

David, there's something wrong with the back end of your car, it seems awful high.

NOBLE:

Nice dice. I bet it will take off in a cloud of rust. The Lone Goof! Hi ho Rust, away!

ANGIE:

Look people, this is your beer, not mine. Somebody's got to move it, I'm willing to help but I'm not going to do it alone. (*No reaction*) Fine, I'll do it alone. But I'll bet if there was a party going on there'd be a flaming trail to the beer.

Angie goes to the beer.

ANDREW:

Mother, I don't want to do this, we shouldn't be doing this, but I don't seem to have any other choice. Just remember, Mom, I'm doing this under protest and …

MARTHA:

Go!

ANDREW:

I'm going, I'm going.

Andrew joins Angie as they repeatedly carry beer cases out to the car. Noble tries to sncak out but finds Martha in front of him.

NOBLE:

Hi.

MARTHA:

And where do you think you're going?

NOBLE:

Like gall stones, time passes. I've got places to go, dances to dance.

Noble walks up to Marianne.

NOBLE:
> Well, I'm outta here. This is it.

Marianne looks up. She turns to David, almost in tears. The phone rings, nobody goes to answer it. It rings again and slowly Martha backs up, not wanting to miss anything.

MARIANNE:
> There's an escape route for every place and situation, David. Here's yours. Come with me. Let's hop in your Camaro and go to Michigan. Just say, what the hell, we're here to burn rubber and gas. Then I'll know there's something still alive in you. What happened last night shows there's still a heartbeat.

NOBLE:
> Wait a minute …

MARTHA:
> (*Answers phone*) Ahneen, make it quick. Two cases, got it, bye.

She hangs up, then something occurs to her.

MARTHA:
> Who was that?

Andrew and Angie walk out carrying beer.

ANDREW:
> Ever wonder who the genius was that named this stuff "light beer"?

Everybody is quiet and Andrew notices this at the doorway.

ANDREW:
> What happened?

Angie bumps into him pushing him out the door.

DAVID:
> You want me to leave? Quit work, just like that? I can't, Marianne. I have responsibilities, obliga-tions. It's not that easy. I've got the council meet-ing on Wednesday, the DIA are bugging me about last month's financial reports, not to men-tion the housing board is planning …

MARIANNE:
> Never mind, David. I didn't think so. One last chance.

NOBLE:
> Actually that's his second-last chance.

DAVID:
> I can't …

> *Marianne starts to leave with Noble. She grabs Andrew and gives him a big bear hug.*

MARIANNE:
> Blue.

ANDREW:
> (*Grunting*) Oh, there goes a rib.

MARIANNE:
> Look after my garden, Blue, and don't get too cocky.

MARTHA:
> Don't use dirty words in my house.

MARIANNE:
> (*To Angie*) Look after him, okay?

> *Marianne approaches Martha. They talk in Ojibway.*

MARIANNE:
> Gdo-zaagin, Mamaa. [I love you, Mom.]

MARTHA:
> Baa-aang waamzin. Ndo-dawendaan ji-bi-mno-giiweyan, ndaan. [You be careful out there. I want you to come home safe and sound, daughter.]

MARIANNE:

(*To David, in English*) I hoped you were alive, David, but I refuse to stay here and bury you.

DAVID:

Marianne, don't go.

MARIANNE:

David, don't stay.

She disappears out the door with Noble.

NOBLE:

I only wanted breakfast.

He exits. Martha fights back tears.

MARTHA:

Keep the beer moving.

Angie and Andrew leave to get more beer.

DAVID:

I didn't think she'd actually do it.

MARTHA:

In my life I've seen two kinds of Indians, those that are happy doing what they do, and those that feel they should be happy but aren't. I think it's every person's journey in life to choose which one they are.

DAVID:

Where do white people fit in?

MARTHA:

God only knows. You still got me.

DAVID:

I guess I do.

Then the phone rings.

MARTHA:

That phone again. Maybe this wasn't such a good idea. My legs are beginning to hurt and you know what they say—once the knees go, your bootlegging career is over. (*Picks up the phone*) Ahneen. (*Pause*) Yes he is. (*To David*) David, it's the band manager. He wants to talk with you.

She holds out the phone as David grabs it.
Angie and Andrew come back into the kitchen.

MARTHA:

You two, come here now.

DAVID:

Yes sir. (*Pause*) Today? But it's a holiday. (*Pause*) I'm really not up to it, I'd rather come in tomorrow if it's possible.

MARTHA:

Mudbin. [Sit down]

DAVID:

Really, I don't think I could handle finishing that report right at the present minute. Frank, can't it wait? (*Pause*) Yes I know it's black fly season in Moose Factory right now.

ANGIE:

Doesn't sound too good.

DAVID:

But … (*Pause*) But… (*Pause*) This isn't really fair, it's a holiday today. (*Pause, then begins to get angry*) You're supposed to be working on the report too, Frankie. (*Pause*) Just a minute, Frankie, you finish the report and I think you know what you can do with it. And I've got one last word for you Frankie Baby, and I want you to think long and hard about it. F.O.A.D. FOAD!

ANDREW:

Foad?

DAVID:
Short for "fuck off and die."

MARTHA:
David!

DAVID:
Sorry Martha, but damn that felt good.

ANDREW:
Atta go David.

David starts running to the door.

DAVID:
If you'll excuse me, I gotta get going.

ANDREW:
Where?

ANGIE:
To Michigan!

DAVID:
That Camaro looks like it has balls, I can probably catch up to them before they hit the highway.

Angie catches him at the door.

ANGIE:
But David, what about all the beer we just put in there, and all the rest we are supposed to deliver? Please don't make me carry it back in. I'll steal the car first.

DAVID:
Damn, I forgot about that.

ANGIE:
Shouldn't we wait until dark to deliver it? Isn't that how they do it in the movies?

ANDREW:
Who are you?

DAVID:
I can't wait. I've got to go as soon as possible if I'm gonna catch them.

MARTHA:
> But you promised us the car.

ANDREW:
> What a fine bunch of bootleggers you are. You have absolutely no idea what you're doing. All right then, fine. If we're gonna do this, and this one time only, let's do this right.

DAVID:
> Andrew, they're getting farther away. It's either now or never.

ANDREW:
> Okay, let's think about this logically. That sign tipped off the police, so we'll have to disguise ourselves and cover our tracks. First of all, transportation. We want to avoid using any car that might be recognized as ours.

ANGIE:
> The Camaro.

ANDREW:
> Right. Fits perfectly, an unknown vehicle.

MARTHA:
> Who would do that to the rear end of a car? It looks like it's in heat.

ANDREW:
> And if we leave now, we can …

DAVID:
> No, I go alone. I don't want to have to bring you all the way back here.

Andrew studies David for a moment.

DAVID:
> What are you looking at? What's he looking at?

MARTHA:
> Blue, what are you looking at?

ANDREW:
Not much to work with.

DAVID:
What?

ANDREW:
David, delivering bootleg beer in a souped up '75 Camaro. Not exactly an inconspicuous sight. He'll stand out like a sore thumb.

DAVID:
A sore what?

ANDREW:
I got an idea. Come on.

They exit to Andrew's room. Angie and Martha remain in the kitchen.

ANGIE:
Think David will catch Marianne?

MARTHA:
Probably.

ANGIE:
Ma'am, as you may have noticed, your son and I have become quite close over the last 24 hours.

MARTHA:
I noticed.

ANGIE:
Of course you did. I hope you approve. He's a very special and intelligent boy.

MARTHA:
I know he is.

ANGIE:
Of course you do. What I mean to say is I like him a lot, and I think he likes me. We would like to see more of each other in the future. We are, after all, practically next-door neighbors.

MARTHA:
I know you are.

There is an uncomfortable silence. Back in the bedroom, Andrew is rummaging through some clothing.

DAVID:

What do you mean I have to wear a disguise? You're blowing this all out of proportion, don't you think?

ANDREW:

Wasn't it you who said something earlier about 30 to 60 days? That can still be arranged, you know. Oh, here it is, try this on.

He tosses David a pair of track pants.

DAVID:

You can't be serious?

ANDREW:

Serious is the difference between a misdemeanor and a felony. (*Selects another piece*) This should help.

Martha enters.

MARTHA:

David, I …

She spots David in his underwear. She hides her eyes.

MARTHA:

I didn't see anything, I didn't see anything.

DAVID:

Martha, it's okay. At least they're clean.

ANDREW:

What did you want, Mom?

MARTHA:

I just wanted to ask David about dropping off the money for the beer. I do not bootleg on the honor system, you know.

DAVID:

Don't worry about it, I'll wire you the money.

MARTHA:

Fine. (*To herself*) Whatever that means, but I trust him.

She exits as Andrew holds up a ratty-looking sweatshirt.

DAVID:

I'd rather go to jail than wear something like that.

Martha reenters the kitchen.

MARTHA:

Now where were we? Oh yes, is Maggie your aunt or not?

ANGIE:

Yes Ma'am, but …

MARTHA:

No buts. Cousins shouldn't be looking at each other that way. You two are related. It ain't right.

ANGIE:

But we're related by marriage only.

MARTHA:

Wait a minute, then … but where does your Aunt Peg fit into all this?

ANGIE:

I don't have an Aunt Peg.

MARTHA:

Must be my Aunt Peg then. Just a moment.

Martha draws some figures in the air, tracing relations and family trees.

MARTHA:

(*Happily*) Angie! Welcome!

ANGIE:

To me scratch.

MARTHA:

That's "ch'meegwetch." [Thank you very much.]

David is finished dressing.

ANDREW:

And the pieces of resistance, ta da.

Andrew pulls out a pair of rubber boots.

DAVID:

(*Resigned*) Why not?

ANDREW:

Better not get in a car accident, you'd be buried as John Doe.

DAVID:

I should be so lucky.

ANDREW:

Grab a few more cases and that should just about fill up your car.

DAVID:

Thank God, I gotta get out of here.

They enter the kitchen.

ANGIE:

David?! You look like a rummage sale exploded.

DAVID:

I know. Martha, can you look after my house while I'm gone? I don't know how long I'll be.

MARTHA:

Don't you worry about that, David, you just skedaddle.

DAVID:

Okay, thanks a lot. I'm outta here.

David almost makes it out the door before Martha calls him.

MARTHA:

The list, the list!

DAVID:

Right, the list.

Andrew hands David the list. David glances at it and laughs.

ANGIE:

What is it?

DAVID:
> Frankie wants three cases of Blue.

ANDREW/ANGIE:
> The band manager?!

DAVID:
> Looks like my job will be waiting for me when I get back. Marianne, here I come. Noble, out you go.
>
> *David exits.*

ANGIE:
> Isn't that terribly romantic?

ANDREW:
> Delivering beer?

ANGIE:
> Why is it men never understand true romance?

ANDREW:
> It gets in the way of good sex.

MARTHA:
> It certainly has been a busy day. I expect to be beerless by dark, if all goes well and it gets hotter.

ANGIE:
> So you and the church are saved.

MARTHA:
> For now. We still got to worry about that new organ. That will cost a fortune. My goodness, look at the time. Do you want to stay for lunch, Angie?

ANGIE:
> I'd love to.

ANDREW:
> Oh Mom, that reminds me, while Angie and me were out earlier, we bumped into Marjorie. She wants to come over for dinner sometime this week. I told her I'd mention it to you.

MARTHA:

There is no way on God's green Earth that I will let that woman into my house.

ANDREW:

Mom, she's your sister.

MARTHA:

Only by blood. Enough about her, you and Angie go out to the garden and pick some fresh peas for me.

ANDREW:

Oh yeah, the garden. Marianne asked me to look after her half. Where exactly is it?

MARTHA:

Out back, to the right, by those sumach trees.

Andrew looks out, his eyes searching, then he discovers the garden. His eyes widen.

ANDREW:

Oh my god!

MARTHA:

That reminds me, Father Belaney was asking about you. Wants to know if you'd help in the organ drive.

ANGIE:

(*To Andrew*) What's wrong?

ANDREW:

(*Pointing*) Over there.

MARTHA:

What are you two mumbling about now?

ANGIE:

Is that what I think it is?

Martha closes the cash box.

MARTHA:
Not nearly enough for a down payment on an organ. That crazy Marjorie wants to get the most elaborate machine available. She always did have a fondness for big organs.

ANDREW:
Look at all of it!

Martha turns around, puzzled by their tone.

MARTHA:
What's so fascinating about my garden?

ANDREW:
Mom, that's grass.

MARTHA:
Imagine that in a backyard.

ANGIE:
No, we mean, like, weed.

MARTHA:
Blue, that's something you can do, weed the garden.

ANDREW:
Mom, that's pot out there, Mary Jane, marijuana.

MARTHA:
Oh, that Marianne and her strange herbs.

Andrew returns to look out the window as Martha ponders.

ANGIE:
There must be a fortune out there.

They've got Martha's attention finally.

MARTHA:
You can sell this stuff?

Andrew and Angie turn their heads slowly to look at Martha.

Lights go down.

THE END

THE BOOTLEGGER BLUES

Narration: "My bootlegging mother."

She's got the blues _____ That ain't no news _____ She's got the

blues _____ 'cause she's sel-lin' them two by two _____ Talk-in' 'bout _____

the Boot-leg-ger Blues _____ She's got t

blues that ain't no news we're talk-in' 'bout the Boot-leg-ger Blues _____

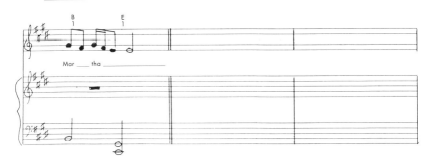

Mar ____ tha _____

Drew Taylor, an Ojibway from the Curve Lake Reserve in Ontario, studied Radio and Television Broadcasting at Seneca College and has gone on to a successful career as a writer for stage and screen. He has written scripts for the tv programs "Street Legal" and "The Beachcombers," and has written and directed several documentary films. His plays have toured many parts of Canada. Drew has also worked as a Native Affairs reporter for CBC Radio, and has written articles on Native arts and culture for *Maclean's, Cinema Canada,* and *Southam News.* He is currently developing a series for CBC-TV based on *The Bootlegger Blues.*

Drew Taylor's first book, Toronto at Dreamer's Rock and Education Is Our Right: Two One-Act Plays was published by Fifth House in 1990.